++
796.357
RS63yam
2009

FOND DU LAC PUBLIC LIBRARY

MAY 1 0 2010

WITHDRAWN

D1649231

BASIC BIOGRAPHIES

Jackie Robinson

by Cynthia Amoroso and Robert B. Noyed

Jackie was born in Georgia on January 31, 1919. His family moved to California when he was a baby.

Jackie played many different sports when he was young.

Jackie's family was poor. His mother worked very hard for her kids.

Jackie is wearing a hat in this family picture.

In school, Jackie enjoyed sports. He was very good at basketball, football, baseball, and track.

Jackie liked to play football.

Jackie played baseball just as well as the players in the major leagues. But he could not join. Black people were not allowed to play major league sports at that time.

Jackie married Rachel Isum in 1946.

Jackie played baseball in the **Negro League**. Then he was asked to join the Brooklyn Dodgers.

Jackie played for the Kansas City Monarchs in the Negro League.

The Dodgers baseball team had only white players. Jackie played his first Major League Baseball game on April 15, 1947.

Jackie was the only black person on his team, the Dodgers.

Jackie's first year on the team was hard. Many people were unkind. They said blacks and whites should not play on the same team. But Jackie played his best.

Jackie had many fans.

Jackie won many awards for baseball. His team won the **World Series** in 1955. Jackie played his last season in 1956.

Jackie won many awards.

Jackie worked hard to make things equal for all people. He died in 1972. People remember him as one of the best baseball players ever.

Jackie made baseball more fair for everyone.

Glossary

league (LEEG): A group of sports teams that play each other are in a league. One baseball league was the Negro League.

major leagues (MAY-jur LEEGS): The top professional baseball leagues are called the major leagues. The Brooklyn Dodgers were in the major leagues.

Negro League (NEE-groh LEEG): The Negro League was a baseball league just for black men. Jackie Robinson played baseball in the Negro League.

World Series (WURLD SEER-eez): The World Series is the set of games each year that decides the best Major League Baseball team. Jackie Robinson's team won the World Series.

To Find Out More

Books
Abraham, Philip. *Jackie Robinson*. Danbury, CT: Children's Press, 2002.

Farrell, Edward. *Young Jackie Robinson*. Mahwah, NJ: Troll Associates, 2003.

Greene, Carol. *Jackie Robinson: Baseball's First Black Major-Leaguer*. Chicago: Children's Press, 1990.

Web Sites
Visit our Web site for links about Jackie Robinson: *childsworld.com/links*

Note to Parents, Teachers, and Librarians: We routinely verify our Web links to make sure they are safe and active sites. So encourage your readers to check them out!

Index

About the Authors

Cynthia Amoroso has worked as an elementary school teacher and a high school English teacher. Writing children's books is another way for her to share her passion for the written word.

Robert B. Noyed has worked as a newspaper reporter and in the communications department for a Minnesota school district. He enjoys the challenge and accomplishment of writing children's books.

On the cover: Jackie Robinson posed at a baseball game in 1946.

Published by The Child's World®
1980 Lookout Drive • Mankato, MN 56003-1705
800-599-READ • www.childsworld.com

ACKNOWLEDGMENTS
The Child's World®: Mary Berendes, Publishing Director
The Design Lab: Design and production
Red Line Editorial: Editorial direction

PHOTO CREDITS: John Lent/AP Images, cover; PhotoDisc, cover, 1, 14; AP Images, 3, 5, 9, 11, 13, 15, 17; Hulton Archive/Getty Images, 7; Marty Lederhandler/AP Images, 19; Jacob Harris/AP Images, 21

Copyright © 2010 by The Child's World®
All rights reserved. No part of this book may be reproduced or utilized in any form or by any means without written permission from the publisher.

Printed in the United States of America in Mankato, Minnesota.
November 2009
F11460

LIBRARY OF CONGRESS CATALOGING-IN-PUBLICATION DATA
Amoroso, Cynthia.
  Jackie Robinson / by Cynthia Amoroso and Robert B. Noyed.
    p. cm. — (Basic biographies)
  Includes index.
  ISBN 978-1-60253-342-4 (library bound : alk. paper)
  1. Robinson, Jackie, 1919-1972—Juvenile literature. 2. Baseball players—United States—Biography—Juvenile literature. 3. African American baseball players—Biography—Juvenile literature I. Noyed, Robert B. II. Title. III. Series.
  GV865.R6A83 2010
  796.357092—dc22 [B]   2009029371